To   Leha

From   mom

new seasons®

New Seasons is a registered trademark of Publications International, Ltd.

Photography from: Shutterstock.com

Louis Weber, CEO
Publications International, Ltd.
8140 Lehigh Avenue
Morton Grove, IL 60053

www.pilbooks.com

Manufactured in China.

8 7 6 5 4 3 2 1

ISBN: 978-1-64030-711-7

Mothers & Daughters

A mother guides her daughter through the steps of childhood.

Mothers give us an extra boost
in the obstacle course of life.

How lucky I am to get to share
your secret family recipes.

Mothers teach us the meaning
of unconditional love.

Mom, thank you for showing me that even the smallest act can help change the world.

You taught me what it means to share.

A mother will always be there to help her daughter weather the storm.

I am blessed to have a mother who takes pride in the strength of her family.

You are my rock when times are hard.

One of a mother's jobs
is to remind her daughter
how sweet life truly is.

Mothers make every milestone
all the more meaningful.

A mother will remind her
daughter to take a jacket,
even when she's all grown up.

Mothers are here to teach their daughters the meaning of sisterhood.

A mom can soothe her daughter's heart with her wise words and gentle touch.

Mom, I love that you give me
the courage to take risks.

Our moms bring out laughter
like no one else can.

I'm so lucky to have a mother
who is happy to share her company,
regardless of what she is doing.

Good mothers teach their daughters
how to find joy everywhere.

A mother nourishes her daughter's body and soul.

Mothers teach us how to have adventures.

Motherhood is showing your daughter
where she comes from and
whom she may become.

Mothers are teachers, showing their daughters when to hold on tight and when to let go.

Encouraging her daughter to let her imagination run wild is one of a mother's most important jobs.

You taught me how to be streetwise.

Mothers make sure we acquire
the knowledge we will need
to face the world on our own.

Mothers show their daughters the importance of a little self-care.

A mother is a constant source
of support and strength.

A mother encourages her daughter to take the first big steps toward her future.

Mothers teach us the importance of tradition.

A mother must remind her daughter that self-worth is based on much more than a pretty face.

My mother showed me that
there's always time to dance.

A daughter is never too old to need her mother.

A girl can always be sure that
one person will handle her heart
with care—her mother.

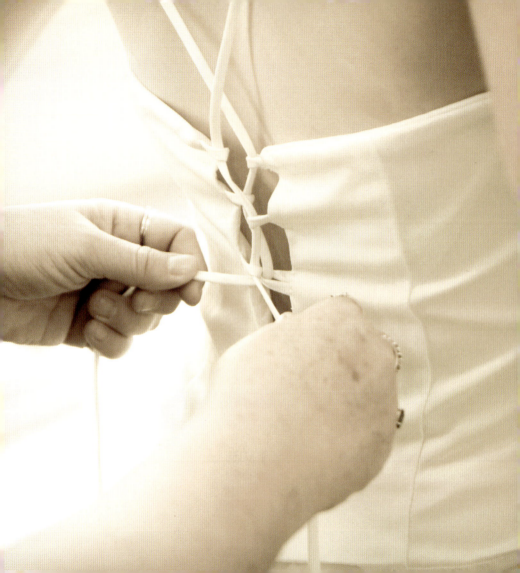

Mom, I need you to stand by me during the important moments of my life.

I learn so much from you.

I love sharing my secrets
and dreams with you.

I count on you to
come home, where I can be safe
in your arms once again.

Thank you for pushing me
to reach my full potential.

Sitting by your side is
my favorite place to be.

A mother teaches her daughter
to sing the song that's in her heart.

Our mother's silly spirit is
her greatest gift to us.

Daughter, may you always dance like no one is watching. Don't take things too seriously.

Mothers know exactly what to say
to make a bad day better.

Mom, teach me how to look for
the beauty in everything.

Thank you for making sure
I always eat my vegetables.

I cherish the simple moments
we spend together.

No one makes me laugh like you do.

Show me how to share
the love you have given me
with the rest of the world.

I wish to have you always by my side.

Snuggled up with you is
the best way to spend a day.

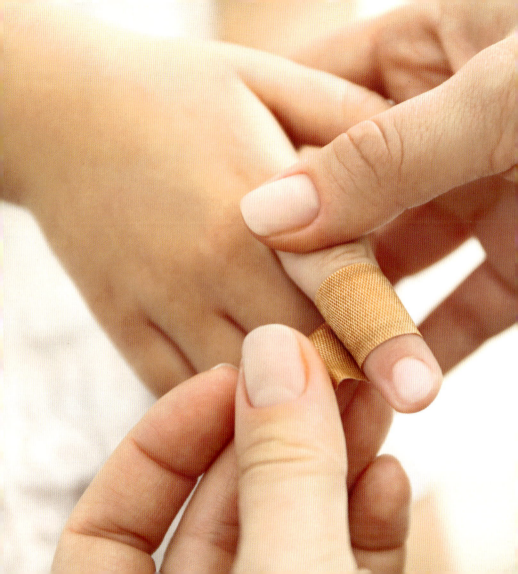

Mothers know just what to do
to make our pain go away.

Mom, I can count on you
to carry me through life.